AF211878

ANN CARLYLE

SACRED CONTRACTS

The Essential Guide on How to Connect With Your Spirituality, Discover What Empowered Spirituality is and How it Can Help You Find Your Faith and Be Happier in Life

Descrierea CIP a Bibliotecii Naţionale a României
ANN CARLYLE
    SACRED CONTRACTS. The Essential Guide on How to Connect With Your Spirituality, Discover What Empowered Spirituality is and How it Can Help You Find Your Faith and Be Happier in Life / Ann Carlyle – Bucharest: Editura My Ebook, 2021
    ISBN

ANN CARLYLE

SACRED CONTRACTS

The Essential Guide on How to Connect With Your Spirituality, Discover What Empowered Spirituality is and How it Can Help You Find Your Faith and Be Happier in Life

My Ebook Publishing House
Bucharest, 2021

TABLE OF CONTENTS

FOREWORD

The best way to be able to develop one's greater spiritual connection can actually be discovered through examining the way that greater connections are created in general. Connecting with your spirituality is something that you cannot do in a day or in an hour; it is something that requires patience, time, consistency, effort and self-discovery. Get all the info you need here.

CHAPTER 1

INTRO

Synopsis

There are many people who erroneously think that they are actually alone in this world – as a matter of fact, all of us are made up of halves; every individual living in this world, no matter what your belief is, has another half who is in existence in the world of spirits. Even though you cannot see it or even sense your other half, bear in mind that you're just one-half of a big whole.

The Basics

The meaning of spirituality means different to every individual. It actually has various meanings depending on the person. For some people, spirituality is all about participating in an organized religion, attending church activities and going to a mosque, synagogue, church, etc.

For some other people, spirituality means something that is personal. Some individuals are getting in touch with their spiritual side by means of prayer, meditation, yoga, a quiet reflection and even long walks in a solemn place.

Whatever you believe and even think truthfully essentially becomes the life's reality in time. Mental repetition and constant meditation of even the same thought, whether positive or negative programs the human mechanism in order to behave and act in accordance to their thought.

Your spiritual journey is actually not a circus and all situations stem from the thinking pattern of all people and in time, their thoughts become reality. Whatever it is that happens in your life is reflecting your thought pattern, so you have to work on yourself. Lift the negative thinking and the heaviness.

Clear all your baggage in life that seems to make things in your life even harder. Remember that clarity always lead to purity and your purity will lead to divinity. Spirituality is not always considered to as philosophy or a religion.

Spirituality is not a matter of debates, discussion or even convenience. It is actually own personal reality and our way of being able to relate to truth.

Spirituality is an important path of being able to go through life truthfully.

Spirituality is a spiritual way of growing and living towards the new and the next lead of growth and development and a way towards self-development.

CHAPTER 2

WHY PEOPLE HAVE NO FAITH TODAY

Synopsis

Faith is actually one of the strangest and strongest emotions of people. Faith is really important for us to grow our spirituality. Faith is mostly defined as the belief at something that doesn't rest on material evidence or on logical proof. Thereby, the source of faith lies not within the human mind that always require evidence and logical explanations, but it lies on the "sixth sense" or "intuition" as well as "gut feeling" that always seem to have no any reason at all.

Losing Faith

Faith is synonymous to trust, however the degree of the latter is even much higher as compared to faith. Trust is mostly recognized with every person whereas faith contains much wider range or spectrum and this may include inanimate creation of human such as religions, principles, etc.

Therefore, thinking through its definition, faith appear as an opposite to science since the very foundation of science is always laid on material or tangible evidence and logic.

Faith is also an emotional state of an individual that uses intuition in order to believe on others or something that you cannot see instead of seeking for proof or evidence. Faith is about believing into something that you cannot actually see. It is believing that something is present even with no tangible evidence is present.

Because of the real nature of faith, many people refuse to believe at some things that they can't see or feel. One of the main reasons why many people are being so unfaithful these days is due to fact that they are searching for material evidence or tangible proofs. They refuse to believe because they cannot see it and there will be no one who can manifest the truthfulness of everything.

In today's life, everything seems to be defined by science; that everything in this world has a scientific reason; that the world was not created by someone. When people got sick and die, it is not because it is their time to die but because their body becomes so weak or the doctors weren't good enough to heal that person. People have no faith today also because of science and they don't accept that there is someone superior above who has the power over everything in this world.

However, there are also some people who once believed and have been faithful, but due to their personal experiences, their faith wavered until they don't believe anymore. Oftentimes, people wonder why God doesn't bless them even when they have really been faithful to Him.

They are starting to cry out load to God for the things they want to nothing really happen. Because of these circumstances, people start to refuse to believe. They start to think that there is no loving God who can give them the things that they want. However, you have to keep in mind that there is also a test of faith.

Faith is also about believing even though things seem to fall apart. If some things are falling apart, continue to be faithful and you will be happy and blessed.

CHAPTER 3

WHAT IS TRUE SPIRITUALITY?

Synopsis

Spirituality is an act of developing and communication with your most essential and greatest identity – you Soul.

True spirituality is a journey if self improvement and self discovery. Many people who are spiritual are starting look within themselves to find our all intricate details of their own identities. Most of us are just living, living without any purpose.

Just wake up in the morning, do their tasks and that would be their daily routines. Spiritual people are also armed with the ever growing and increasing knowledge of who they actually are. Those individuals who are spiritually enthusiastic attempt to improve and develop on that identity since they want to make their soul even stronger.

True Spirituality

True spirituality lies in every individual because each individual has a soul. How much you are trying to connect with your soul is always up to you and how much you decide to develop your soul is likewise up to you. Bear in mind that these are spiritual acts and your own path in life is always your personal spiritual journey.

There are some people who believe that spirituality is religion, but you have to bear in mind that spirituality is actually the opposite of a religion. Religion is just the same concept for every individual who is involved in it.

A person's spirituality is always unique, and having said that, spirituality is always different for each person all over the world since our souls are at different stages and levels of development. Every individual has a deep-level weaknesses and strengths and this is the main reason why spirituality is actually not a religion.

It might be safe to say that every individual has been in a situation where they are thinking of their real purpose in this life and they also thought that they are no longer doing what they should be in their lives. It could just require some changes that they need in order to complete their life-altering changes.

It is actually our nature to doze off in the wrong path every now and then, just so we can be fully aware of our main purpose, direction and path really is. By creating some spiritual connections to be able to get heading and redefine your path in the most perfect direction will give you an assurance that you are starting to act from your real self and not all about out of desperation to make a change.

True spirituality is sometimes one of the main aspects that can help every individual to know and deeply understand their main purpose in life.

CHAPTER 4

WHAT IS THE EMPOWERED SPIRITUALITY MINDSET?

Synopsis

There are so many questions today that relate to the empowerment of spirituality mindset.

Well, an empowered spirituality mindset is always being faithful, positive and always believing that even things are starting to fall apart, or even though things may fall the way that you do not want them to be, you always have hope and faith that your life's dark side will soon come to an end.

Having an empowered spiritual mindset can become of the main life enhancers that we can have. Many eminent and successful people in this world have actually attained some great levels of spiritual empowerment.

What Is It

Defining an Empowered Spirituality Mindset

Empowered Spiritual Mindset is all about the power to be able to achieve great happiness and success in life. This also provides all people the knowledge in taking their power for them to live a life to their most potential.

An empowered spirituality mindset is also about knowing your roles in the society and understanding what you can do in order to bring about positive changes in your life, in others, in the community as well as in the environment. If you have the ability to empower your spiritual mindset, then it is freedom and independence in whatever facet of life that would just be within your reach.

What Does it Mean By having an Empowered Spiritual Mindset?

Spiritual empowerment is actually a sense of freedom that all people always want to attain. Being free and independent in whatever facet in life may surely boost our confidence and also makes us to do even the best in life.

Having an empowered spiritual mindset is also about being motivated to do many things even those that seem to be so impossible. It is also about being highly motivated to accomplish your tasks in a very positive manner.

Having an empowered spiritual mindset also allow the person to see and be more aware of the limitations and capabilities that he possesses. This also makes an individual to become contented and happy with the kind of person that he is right now and striving to develop his/herself to turn his weaknesses into strengths and become successful in life. Being empowered spiritually enables us to become more aware of what really makes us happy and be sensitive to other people.

Understanding the world and knowing one's self are the most essential steps to empowering your spiritual mindset. It is very important to know yourself and everything around you to have an empowered spiritual mindset for your great success.

Moreover, having an empowered spirituality mindset does not really mean being hooked to a certain religion or any religious group so to speak. An empowered spirituality means that your consciousness is finally awakened.

This allows you to see the kind of person you are and being fully aware of the things that you can do for yourself as well to others and the community. It is also your ability to recognize your strengths and weaknesses and lean to become contented with your life.

Becoming spiritually empowered allows you to become more aware of the things that can make you happy. This will also allow an individual to become more sensitive about the things that can make other individuals happy.

Also, if you want to enrich your spirit, it is mostly important to always be motivated. You should never give easily even when things seem to become so complicated.

No matter what aspect of life is actually involved and no matter what the circumstances may be, a person who has an empowered spirituality mindset will always seek to learn and understand more a lot of things in order to make the world a better place for his surroundings and to himself.

CHAPTER 5

TRADITIONAL SPIRITUAL IDEAS VS NEW AGE IDEAS

Synopsis

Understanding the Traditional Spiritual Ideas

Many people in different parts of the world are shaped by their cultures, religion and community that is why a lot of people have different perceptions about spirituality. When it comes to traditional spiritual ideas, some people think about the idea of a unique spiritual realm, something that set apart or it is something about the physical world. The spirituality varieties are thereby to a tremendous extent variety of dualism. Many people have this intuition that people and the world where they live are two distinct natures; one that is immaterial and one that is physical.

Part of the traditional ideas is actually our fear of death and this is producing a dualism of spirit and body, of the supernatural and the natural. Also, another prominent characteristic of a traditional spirituality revolves around the ultimate purpose in life; that people are all here in earth to become tested, refined and to become worthy to live a life with eternal happiness. It is also about a belief that the existence of every individual has a meaning and we are all here in the world because we all have a role to play.

New Ideas

Part of the traditional spiritual idea is the concept of God being the supreme individual, so as people suffer and experience pain in life, people always find a consolation in the knowledge that they are all part of a grand design. One idea of the traditional spiritual is that life has a meaning because an agent (God) endows life with meaning.

Taking a Closer Look at the New Age Ideas

The New Age Ideas of spirituality are terms that are encompassing various concepts which are also derived from different sources which, for over millions of centuries have been contradicting one another. For some people, a New Age is a term that may actually describe the different phenomena which are not normal.

Therefore, the New Age refers to many different concepts which are not normal to almost all of humanity in today's time.

The New Spiritual ideas are those types of spirituality which is not the rule in today's present culture where people live, no matter where you, whether you live at south or north part of the equator.

One of the salient new age ideas is actually the absence of a set of proposition or creed for people to believe in. whereas each institutional religion has an essential creed to be able to stand by, the new age spiritual ideas doesn't actually have creeds. Another idea is the assertion of a certain God who is so different from a God of various established religions. The God of many established religions like Islam, Buddhism and Christianity is actually a transcended God who is beyond their mind to consider, and God who people cannot really experience by their own powers.

The God of the New Age is god who is actually with the universe. He might actually be regarded as the universe itself. He isn't transcended.

24

The Traditional spiritual ideas and the new ideas are actually totally different from each other. Spirituality is unique and it is something personal. Whichever idea you may accept, so long as it will make you a better person, there is no wrong about it.

Although these two ideas are totally different from each other, it is important to just understand them. Whatever idea you have, so long as you are happy with it and you are not hurting others, just continue believing.

CHAPTER 6

WHAT DOES EMPOWERMENT FOR SPIRITUALITY MEAN TO YOU (HOW TO SET GOALS)

Synopsis

Empowerment for spirituality has different meanings. Every individual has different needs and requirements in life that is why they also have created different meaning to their spiritual empowerment. And because all humans are actually needy and they are perpetually requiring help in order to navigate their life, the spiritual empowerment that they often seek may take on various forms.

Since every individual has a unique needs, empowerment for spirituality means setting a goal and paying attention to the most important aspect in your life. Setting goals will always be a part of spiritual empowerment. This is also considered as a very essential part of positive accomplishments and success in life. Those people who are setting goals are being able to know and

26

understand themselves, which is the greatest essence of spiritual empowerment – to be able to fully recognize yourself and be motivated to obtain great success in your life.

Your Goals

Those who set their goals are literally creating maps of their targeted achievement and goals in life, marking on the way where they should start, where to pause, which area to delve a bit and when and where to stop.

Empowerment for spirituality means creating a map that will lead you towards the right path or direction on where you should go. This is also the best way that you can do to be able to connect with your spirituality.

Ways to Set your Goals Towards Empowerment for Spirituality

The confidence required in goal setting is important to spiritual empowerment. Goal setting reveals that you believe in your capabilities to fulfill your goals and accomplish the things that you have set out for yourself.

In order to successfully set your goals, it is important to understand yourself and know your limitations, strengths and weaknesses. Determine what you can and can't do but always believe in yourself that whatever you made or whatever goals you have set, you can always achieve it.

Understand more your surroundings. Spiritual empowerment with goal setting will allow you to take full responsibility for your actions.

Once you have understood your surroundings, you can also create your goal that would be more beneficial not only for you, but also to your environment. This can also help you decide or make decisions about your life.

Know the most important things that you have to put on top of your priorities. This is one of the most important ways that you can do in order to successfully set your goals in life. Once you are able to determine your priorities in your life, you are able to make an essential map for yourself.

Empowerment for spirituality has several meaning and one of the most essential things that would define it is your ability to set your goals and being able to achieve it.

The key benefit of goal setting is achieving your targets and fulfilling your dreams. This will also help you to keep track of your own progress. Setting goals and obtaining them will also help you not just to empower your spirituality, but also improve your self confidence.

CHAPTER 7

WHY ADOPT THE EMPOWERMENT MINDSET FOR SPIRITUALITY?

Synopsis

The empowerment mindset for spirituality will help a person to become a better individual who knows his capabilities, his strengths and who is able to fulfill all his goals in life. Having an empowered mindset for spirituality is also very helpful for a person to help others and to stay positive no matter how bad situations might be. These are actually just some of the primary reasons to adopt the empowerment mindset for spirituality. This is for the growth of the person, personal development, as well as self fulfillment.

Why Do It

Empowerment Mindset for Spirituality – Your Perfect Guidance

Once you set both your feet on the ground, you may always feel confused about the right direction to go and the right path to follow. You may also wonder if you have wandered off the right path along the way. Maybe you have a very complex decision to make. If you are struggling from any of these situations, you need the right guidance. Adopting an empowerment mindset for spirituality will help you discover the right path that will lead you towards success and real happiness. Having an empowered mindset for spirituality will give you a sense of peace with regards to the right decision to make.

Empowerment Mindset for Spirituality – to Bring Strength

Having an empowered mindset will help you in times that you feel weak. This will actually give you enough strength and courage to face every day with smile. Having an empowered mindset will also help you to look at the brighter side of life, that even when things seem to fall on the other direction, you will always still be positive about life. God may also quicken your spirit so that you can feel experience a greater urgency about getting all your tasks done.

Empowerment Mindset for Spirituality – Gives Right Authority

One of the main reasons to adopt Empowerment Mindset for Spirituality is that it will give you right authority. Empowerment always finds its great manifestation in many different ways which are actually subtle. Jesus did not give his disciples many spiritual gifts, however, what he did was to give them impossible tasks to be performed and have given them an authority that they required in order to accomplish the task. Everyone of us, as followers of God has the same authority. An individual may discover that he is empowered to accomplish many things as he step out in faith and be able to use it.

CHAPTER 8

TIPS FOR BECOMING EMPOWERED
FOR SPIRITUALITY

Synopsis

Most of the time, many people allow their mindset to be determined and shaped by all their adversaries and problems in life instead of doing the opposite.

What really happens in this situation is that they are creating a vicious cycle of negative seed thoughts that will lead to negative fruit outcomes.

In times like this, what can you actually do to become empowered for spirituality with regard of the negative events that are being manifested in your life?

By following the right tips for becoming empowered for spirituality will help you become more motivated with your life no matter how bad circumstances may be.

Doing It Right

- *Focus your Empowerment Mindset on Success*

If you want to always become empowered spiritually, always believe that you can obtain great success that you want and just focus your attention into that idea. Every day, you have to remind yourself that you will always succeed no matter what happens and whoever comes in your way. If you have this state of mind, you will obtain greater outcomes than you have every expected.

- *Steer Clear of Failure thinking and Negativity*

Once you surround yourself with all negativities – negative conversation, negative self-talk, you will also attract same negativity in your life and in your experience. Start moving away from all of it. Shift your negative self-talk and negative thinking and become positive. Once you do this, you will see positive changes in your life.

- *Get Busy about Moving Towards your Goal*

In order to stay empowered for spirituality, you have to start getting busy and wrapping yourself up with your goals in life right now. Remember that goal setting is part of an empowered spirituality, so if you continue to do so, you will see the great positive changes that it can happen in your life. If you want to achieve something, sitting around and just waiting is not really an answer to get your desired results.

- *Continue Learning and Educating yourself*

There is really nothing wrong about bind faith, however, since you want to grow and empower your spirituality, the best thing that you can do is to continue learning and always educate yourself. Learn more about belief and religious system. Feed yourself with the words of God. Surf the web, read the scriptures, watch spiritual TV programs and always seek out various religious leaders who can actually provide essential information on various religions.

- *Make Connections with Other People*

Remember that God is working through people in order to make essential things happen. Although it is true that you can grow or empower your spirituality alone, joining together with some people who have great faith can also develop your faith as well as your spiritual awakening and growth.

- *Get all your Goals Clearly Set*

When you say that you want to obtain all the best in life, you are now having a clear mindset of your goals. It is not enough to say that you will be successful in the near future; it is a must to climb your way towards great success. The main thing that you have to do is to understand whether your goal is worth all your efforts, and eliminate the things that will hinder you from obtaining those goals.

Always being empowered for spirituality or being in tune with the spirit require effort and discipline. These tips will help you become more empowered for spirituality and be happy with your life. These are also the primary keys that you can use to obtain real success and happiness.

CHAPTER 9

THE GOOD AND BAD ABOUT THE EMPOWERMENT MINDSET FOR SPIRITUALITY

Synopsis

There are many underlying principles when it comes to empowerment that is why several people also have various perceptions with regards to this concept. The empowerment mindset for spirituality means several things to many people so it also carries several advantages and disadvantages to some individuals.

The Good And Bad

The Good things about the Empowerment Mindset for Spirituality

Having an empowered mindset for spirituality is actually essential because it gives people a tool to progress in their

36

relationships. Empowerment mindset for spirituality is about being happier and living better. This also gives people a more potential to be able to reach out to other people and to love another person.

An empowerment mindset for spirituality is also essential in converting your weaknesses into great strengths. For some people, their weaknesses are those that deprived them of doing things that they want. These are their inferiorities and insecurities that lead them to downfall. However, you have to remember that your weakness will never stay as your weakness. This can also become a perfect tool that can help you develop your weaknesses and turn them into strengths.

Having an empowered mindset for your spirituality also plays a vital role in your overall wellness. Once you believe in something that is greater than yourself and living and developing the values of your beliefs, you will not only improve the wellness of your life, but also improve the lives of many people around you. When you deepen your spirituality and provide spiritual connections, you will also develop yourself.

Empowering your mindset for spirituality is not all about deepening your beliefs and faith, it is also about growing your inner spirit that is important in loving more yourself and other people around. This will also give you a great connection with your mind and body.

The Bad Things about the Empowerment Mindset for Spirituality

Although empowerment of mindset for spirituality is really essential and it offers several benefits, there are also some important considerations that you have to take note of.

For some individuals, the empowerment mindset for spirituality is an overwhelming process. There are also some people who cannot fully understand its real concept that is why all their spiritual empowerment endeavors are starting to be in vain.

Well, the bad thing about the empowerment mindset for spirituality only lies within the mind of the person. This is a positive and advantageous activity, however those who cannot fully understand its concepts and the principles that lie within it, everything seems so complicated. Having an empowered mindset is something that is positive, but if an individual cannot really decipher its real meaning and significance, then the bad things and worst situations happen.

CHAPTER 10

CONCLUSION

Connecting with your spirituality is a process that involves effort, consistency and patience. It is something that needs great attention to be able to fulfill and deeply understand its real meaning.

There are a lot of sources that we can use to able to develop our spirituality and empower our mindset for spirituality. It is actually all about learning about the right things to do and having the right purpose in doing so.

Empowering your spirituality is not all about deepening and growing your beliefs as well as your faith, but it is also about developing your inner spirit. It is also about believing in yourself, loving people and the entire world around you.

Now is the time to strip away all the doubts and unfaithfulness that we feel and replace them with appreciation and love. Having an empowered spirituality will help you rediscover the great power and strength of your own spirit as well as recognize all the greatness of everything around you.

By doing all these things, you can connect reconnect with your spirituality and find your faith. This is also highly necessary for your spirituality to deepen and to grow.

Always remember that essential connection among the body, the mind and the spirit. Through making an essential effort to deepen, develop and empower your spirit, you also improve your mental and physical health and your overall wellness, thereby contributing to a healthier and happier life.

Changing your life and connecting with your spirituality may always seem a very overwhelming and frustrating experience. However, it does not really have to be very complicated. By following the right strategies and steps for spiritual empowerment, you can experience a joy in your life and your life will be transformed in a very positive manner.

There too many questions and concerns with regards to spiritual empowerment. This is actually because empowering one's spirituality and having a spiritual connection can become of the most beneficial life enhancers that can make great changes in our lives.

Printed by Libri Plureos GmbH in Hamburg, Germany